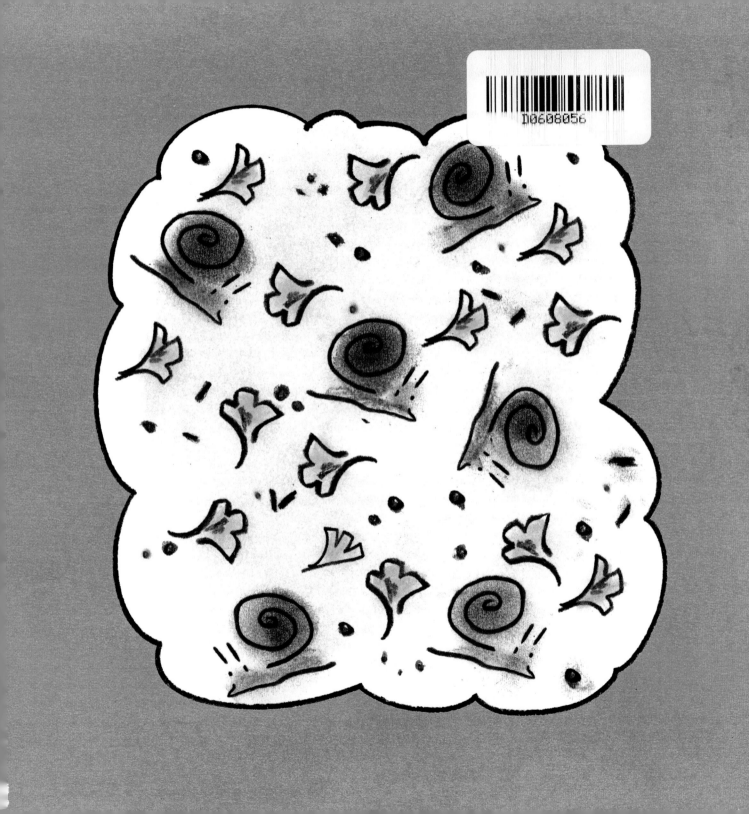

How to Draw a Happy WITCH

and **99** Things that Go BUMP in the Night

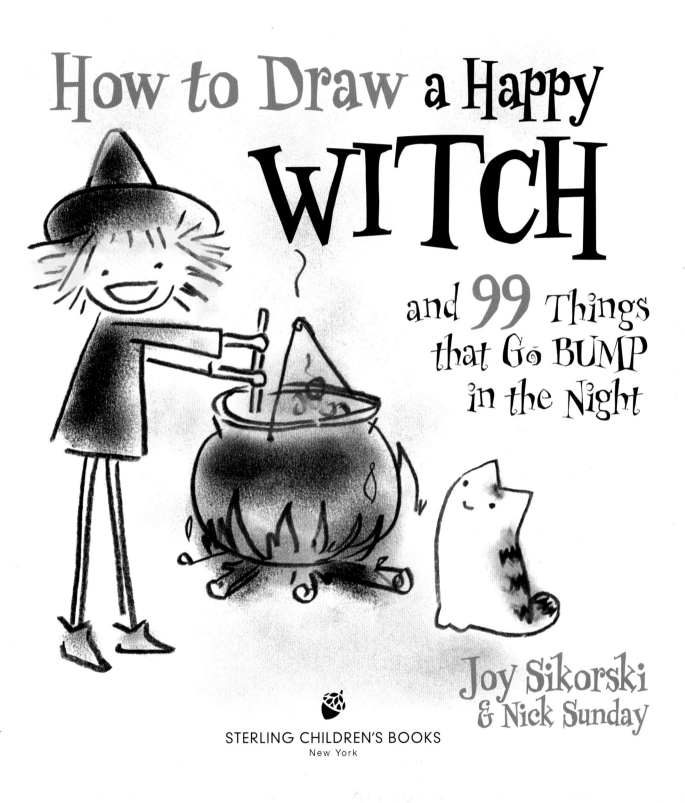

Joy Sikorski
& Nick Sunday

STERLING CHILDREN'S BOOKS
New York

To Elizabeth, Nicholas, and Nancy

STERLING CHILDREN'S BOOKS
New York

An Imprint of Sterling Publishing
387 Park Avenue South
New York, NY 10016

STERLING CHILDREN'S BOOKS and the distinctive Sterling Children's Books logo are registered trademarks for Sterling Publishing Co., Inc.

Lot #:
2   4   6   8   10   9   7   5   3   1
04/11

Distributed in Canada by Sterling Publishing
c/o Canadian Manda Group, 165 Dufferin Street
Toronto, Ontario, Canada M6K 3H6
Distributed in the United Kingdom by GMC Distribution Services
Castle Place, 166 High Street, Lewes, East Sussex, England BN7 1XU
Distributed in Australia by Capricorn Link (Australia) Pty. Ltd.
P.O. Box 704, Windsor, NSW 2756, Australia

The artwork for this book was created using pencil, pastels, and a Mac.

Sterling ISBN 978-1-4027-5708-2

For information about custom editions, special sales, premium and
corporate purchases, please contact Sterling Special Sales
Department at 800-805-5489 or specialsales@sterlingpublishing.com.

www.sterlingpublishing.com/kids

Introduction

Dear Reader,

Little Man is an adventuresome cat who lives on the edge of the wetlands. In this story you will accompany him on a nighttime walk, and you'll learn how to draw just about everything he finds along the way.

Near his house Little Man hears strange noises. Bumpy nighttime noises always mean something mysterious and fun to draw.

Little Man goes to a wonderful place far into the wetland forest. On his way, he meets lots of friendly animals, and we will learn how to draw them all!

Bring your favorite nighttime colors.

Love,
Joy & Nick

The sun begins to rise. Little Man has been out all night long. Scarecrow stands in the hilltop pumpkin patch looking down as if to say, "Good mornin', Little Man."

witch-ity   witch-ity

How to Draw a
Common Yellowthroat
The call of this sulking masked warbler of the wetlands is:
witch-ity, witch-ity, witch-ity.

1.   **2.**   **3.**   **4.**

Little Man Standing and Sitting

1.

2.

3.

4.

5.

6.

1.

2.

3.

4.

Little Man Napping and Jaunting About

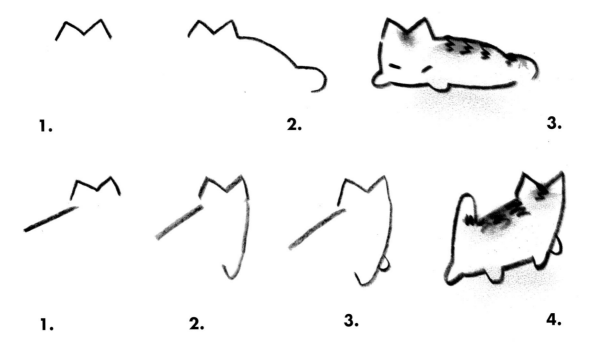

1. 2. 3.

1. 2. 3. 4.

1. 2. 3. 4.

How to Draw a
Scarecrow

1.

2.

3.

4.

5.

6.

7.

How to Draw a
Crow

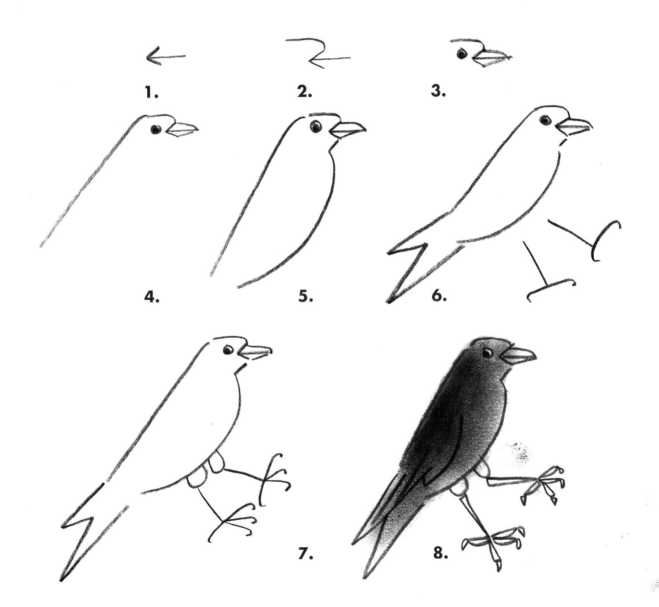

1.

2.

3.

4.

5.

6.

7.

8.

How to Draw the
Apple-Picker's Ladder

1.

2.

3.

4.

Bonus:
apple crate

1.

2.

Notice the handles

3.

squeak! chip!

4.

How to Draw a
Hedgehog
Did you know? Hedgehogs are very noisy.

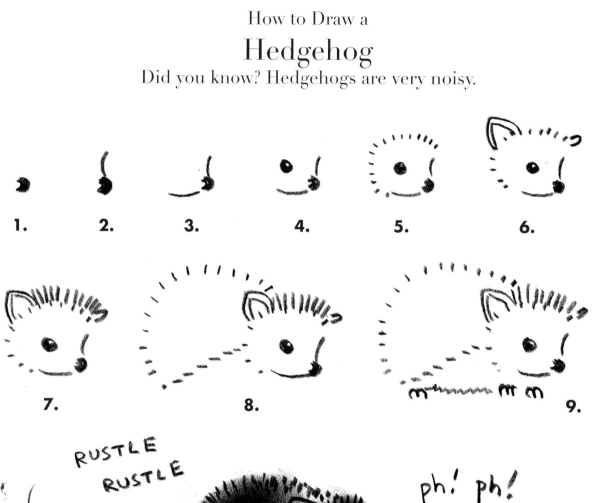

1.　**2.**　**3.**　**4.**　**5.**　**6.**

7.　　**8.**　　**9.**

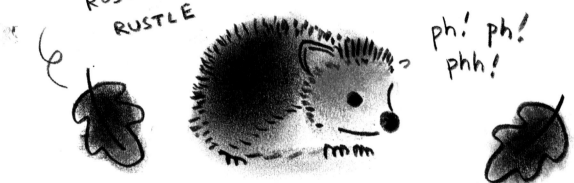

RUSTLE
RUSTLE

ph! ph!
phh!

10.

How to Draw
Autumn Leaves
Shhhhhhh . . . listen to the whispering leaves.

1.

2.

3.

Sugar Maple

Tulip

White Oak

Red Oak

Sassafras

Yellow Poplar

shhhhhh

How to Draw a
Chipmunk

1.

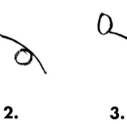

2.

3.

4.

5.

6.

7.

8.

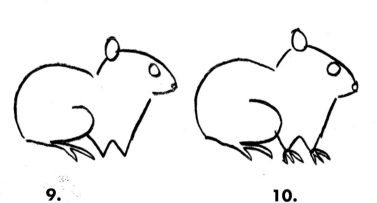

9.

10.

Squeak chip!

11.

How to Draw a
Snail and a Fox
Snails are relatively quiet creatures, whereas foxes bark like dogs.

1. 2. 3. 4. 5.

6. 7. 8.

1. 2. 3. 4.

5. 6. 7.

How to Draw a
Fox Costume

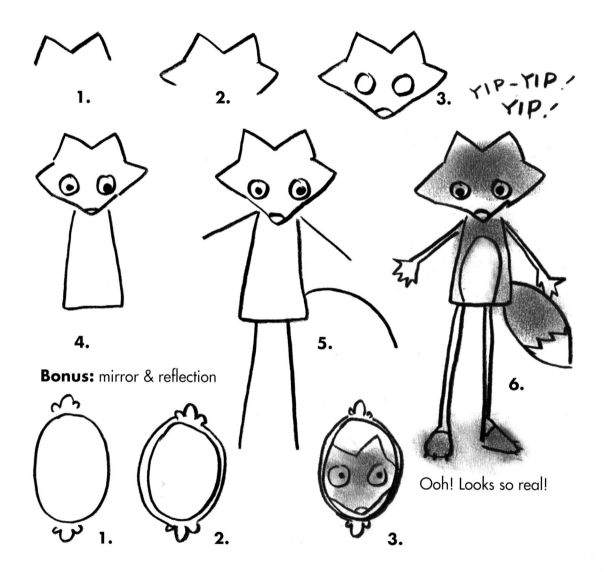

1.

2.

3.

YIP-YIP!
YIP!

4.

5.

6.

Bonus: mirror & reflection

1.

2.

3.

Ooh! Looks so real!

16

As the sun comes up above the sea, Little Man
reaches his house at the edge of the wetlands.

How to Draw a
Bathrobe and Slippers

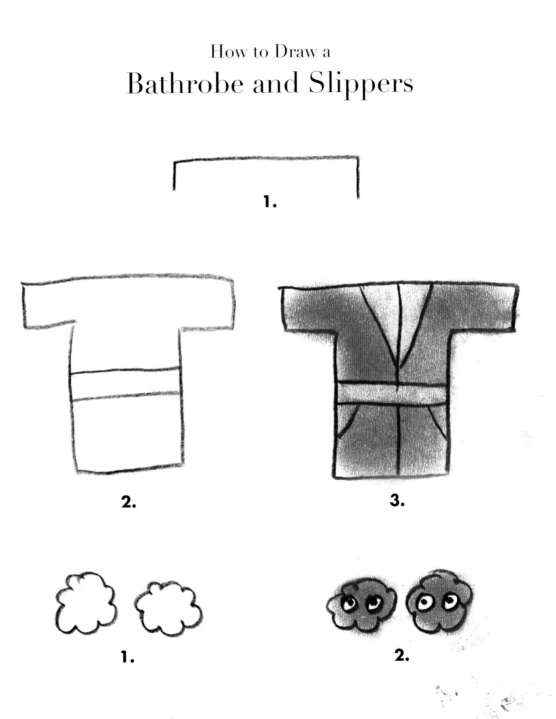

1.

2.

3.

1.

2.

How to Draw a
Moth and a Lightning Bug

Little Man hunting a moth and a lightning bug.

Little Man takes a nap and dreams about the Happy Witch.

In Little Man's dream
she is cooking his favorite
French dish: escargot!

23

How to Draw a
Cooking Pot and Parsley

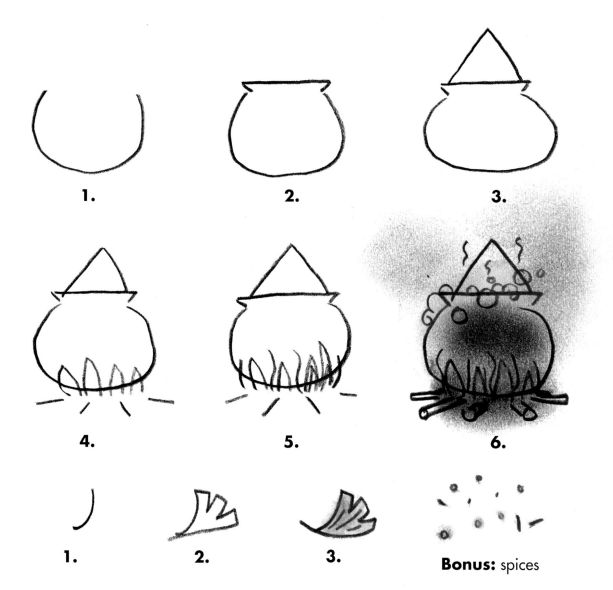

1.

2.

3.

4.

5.

6.

1.

2.

3.

Bonus: spices

Little Man dreams yummy dreams all day.
As night falls, he wakes to the sound of the doorbell ringing.

How to Draw a
Witch and Broom

1.   2.   3.   4.   5.

6.   7.   8.

1.   2.   3.   4.

When the door opens, funny creatures shout,
"TRICK OR TREAT!"

How to Draw a
Ghost Costume

1.

2.

3.

4.

Everybody is dressed in their Halloween costumes.

How to Draw a
Jack-o'-Lantern
A candle burns within the jack-o'-lantern giving it a lovely light.

1.

2.

3.

4.

5.

6.

How to Draw
Different Jack-o'-Lantern Faces

Horrified

Happy

Devilish

Suspicious

Disappointed

Scary

How to Draw
Candy

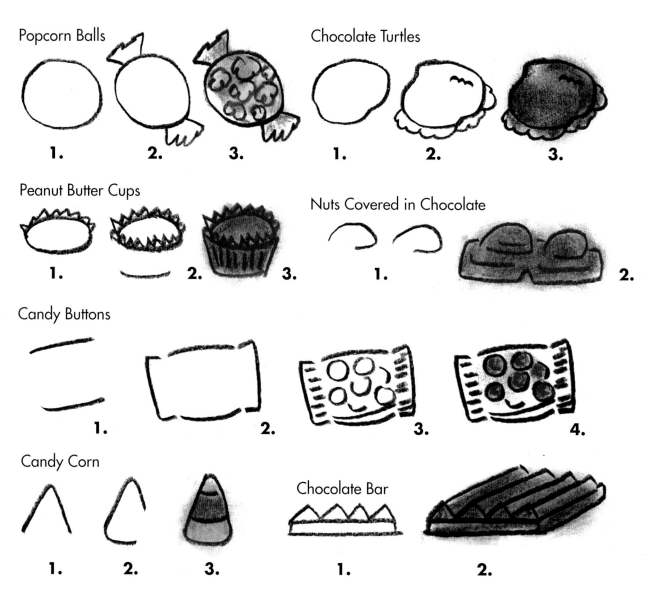

Popcorn Balls

1. **2.** **3.**

Chocolate Turtles

1. **2.** **3.**

Peanut Butter Cups

1. **2.** **3.**

Nuts Covered in Chocolate

1. **2.**

Candy Buttons

1. **2.** **3.** **4.**

Candy Corn

1. **2.** **3.**

Chocolate Bar

1. **2.**

The last trick-or-treaters have left and everyone
has gone to bed. Little Man investigates
the noises around the house.

There's something on top of the curtains.

How to Draw a
Hamster
(front & side view)

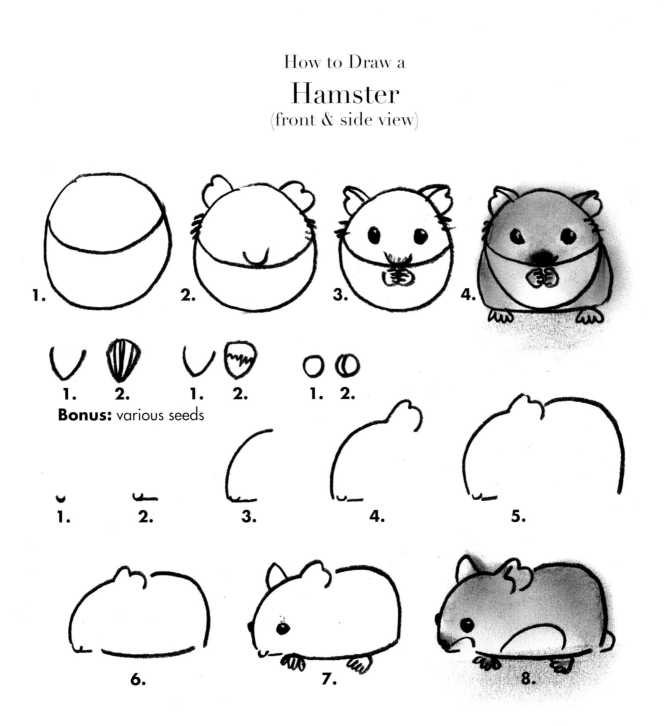

1.

2.

3.

4.

1. 2.

1. 2.

1. 2.

Bonus: various seeds

1. 2. 3. 4. 5.

6. 7. 8.

Little Man chases the wayward hamster back to his house.

How to Draw a
Hamster House

1.

2.

3.

4.

5.

6.

PING!

7.

It's too late for such noisy activities.
Little Man is let out into the night.

Little Man looks around at the colors of the night in the wetlands.

The night is alive with all kinds of mysterious noises.

How to Draw a
Cricket
(top & side view)

1.

2.

3.

4.

5.

cheep cheep! cheep cheep!

1.

2.

3.

4.

5.

chip-chip! chip-chip!

41

How to Draw a
Field Mouse (front view) and a Weed

1.

2.

3.

4.

5.

6.

RUSTLE
RUSTLE

1.

2.

Bonus: a nut.

1.

2.

3.

4.

How to Draw a
Field Mouse (side view)

1.

2.

3.

4.

5.

6.

POINK!
POINK!
POINK!

Little Man investigates. *Poink, Poink, Poink*
is the dripping of the outdoor water faucet.

Bonus: a rose

1. **2.** **3.** **4.**

TAP
TAP
TAP
TAP

Oh! There's the toy car that was lost in the summer time!

Tap, Tap, Tap is the sound of the wind blowing branches against the window.

45

Just as Little Man hears one trick-or-treater say to the other, "Let's go towards town," he meets a porcupine.

How to Draw a
Porcupine

1.

2.

3.

4.

5.

6.

7.

8.

Little Man hears a thump as he walks through the orchard.
He remembers to beware of falling apples. The nighttime
animals are about, and they are very busy.

How to Draw a
Raccoon

1.

2.

3.

4.

5.

6.

7.

8.

9.

10.

11.

Little Man sees Scarecrow pointing to a path
in the woods and hears, "Who cooks for you?"

How to Draw a
Barred Owl
The Barred Owl's call is: *Who cooks for you?*

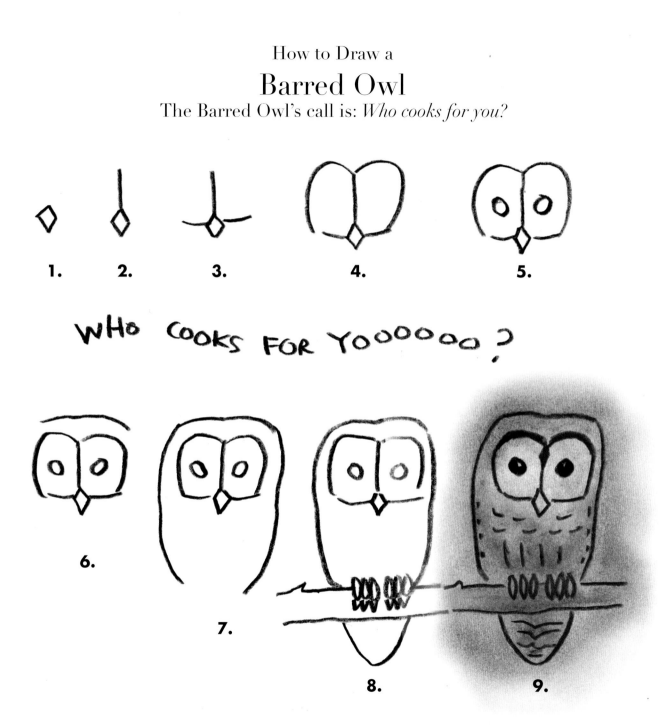

1.   2.   3.   4.   5.

WHO COOKS FOR YOOOOOOO ?

6.

7.

8.

9.

52

How to Draw a
Flying Barred Owl

Little Man meets a skunk and passes him quietly.

How to Draw a
Skunk

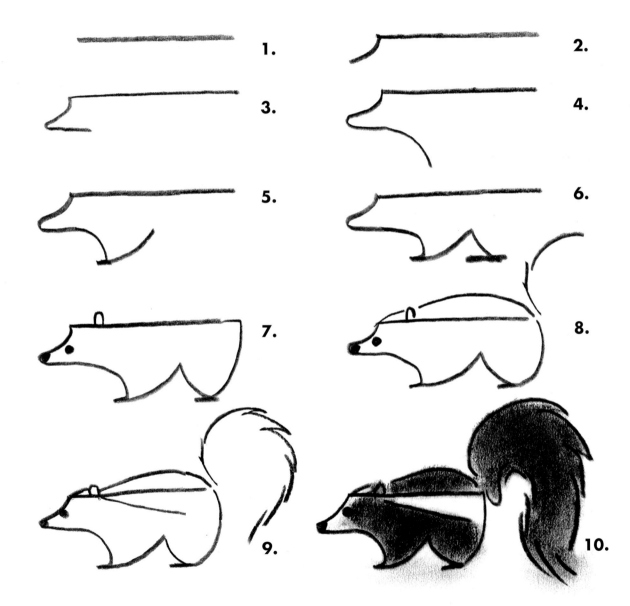

1.

2.

3.

4.

5.

6.

7.

8.

9.

10.

Along the river the shadows flicker and
dance. There's a very loud splashing noise.

How to Draw a
River Otter
Tip: Start with wave shape.

1.

2.

3.

4.

5.

6.

7.

8.

EEEEE!

How to Draw an
Opossum
The opossum family is playing in the trees. It's a midnight romp.

1.   2.   3.   4.   5.

6.   7.   8.

9.   10.

Coyote and its Howl

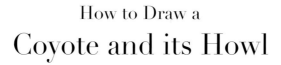

A baby coyote is called a whelp

How to Draw
Wind in the Big Tree

1.

2.

3.

CRASH

CRISH
CRISH

4.

At night the leaves on the trees sound louder than they do in the daytime. There are noises from things moving through the leaves, too.

Tip: Turn book upside down to see the spooky shadow face.

S·C·R·E·E·E·E·K

The full moon makes very spooky shadows.

How to Draw
Moon Shadows

1.

2.

3.

How to Draw a
Deer Portrait and a Wood Mouse

1. 2. 3.

1. 2. 3. 4. 5.

How to Draw a
Deer

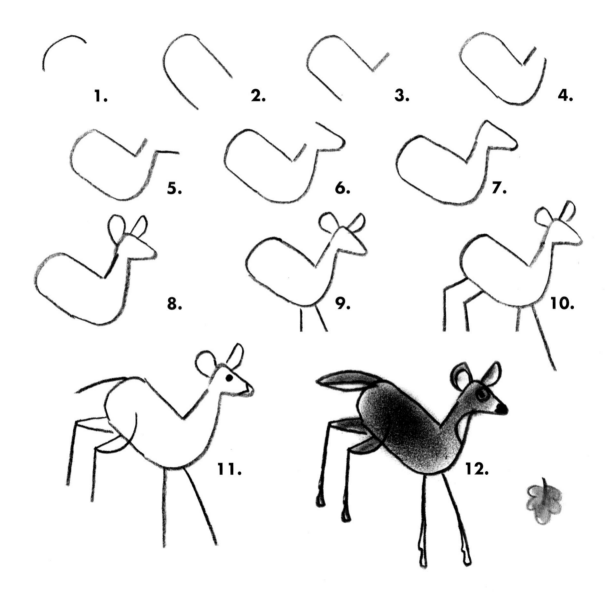

1.

2.

3.

4.

5.

6.

7.

8.

9.

10.

11.

12.

How to Draw a
Night Hawk and a Tasty Bug
The Night Hawk calls: *pork-'n-beans! pork-'n-beans!*

How to Draw a
Whippoorwill
The Whippoorwill calls its name.

whip-poor-will! whip-poor-will!
whip-poor-will! whip-poor-will!
whip-poor-will! whip-poor-will!

1.

2.

3.

4.

5.

How to Draw a
Bat

1.

2.

3.

4.

5.

6.

7.

8.

9.

A gigantic, beautiful green luna moth flutters past
Little Man just as he arrives at Le Chat Noir Bistro.

How to Draw
Le Chat Noir Bistro
(The Black Cat Bistro)

1.

2.

3.

4.

5.

Little Man always stops to look at the black cat on the sign.

It's the night of the Halloween Costume Ball!

74

Monsieur Fox, the head waiter, comes
out to invite Little Man into the kitchen.

How to Draw a
Painting in a Frame

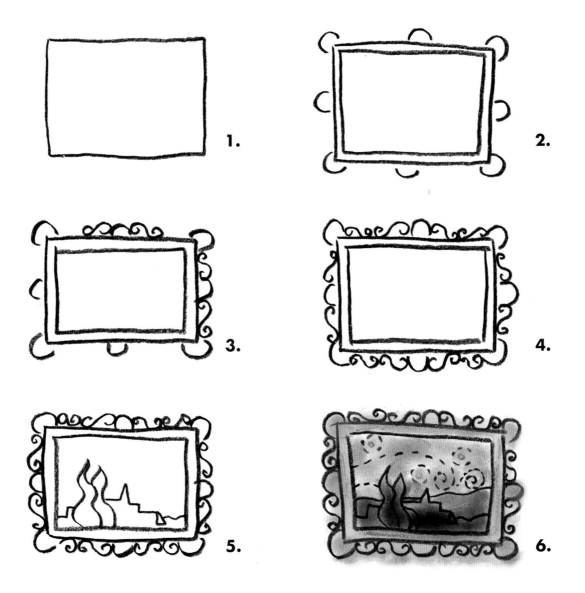

1.

2.

3.

4.

5.

6.

Three Chef Hats, an Apron, and Chef Pants

Chef's hat with pleats

1.   **2.**   **3.**   **4.**   **5.**

Be a pro: The chef's hat is called a toque. The pleats in the toque tell how many ways the chef knows to cook an egg. There are 100 ways to cook an egg!

hat   **1.**   **2.**   **3.**

apron

1.   **2.**   **3.**

chef pants

hat

1.   **2.**   **3.**

The Happy Witch recites a recipe in French
as Little Man translates it into English.

How to Draw a
Grater, a Cake Pan, Frosting Tools, Cake on a Cake Plate, and a Slice of Cake

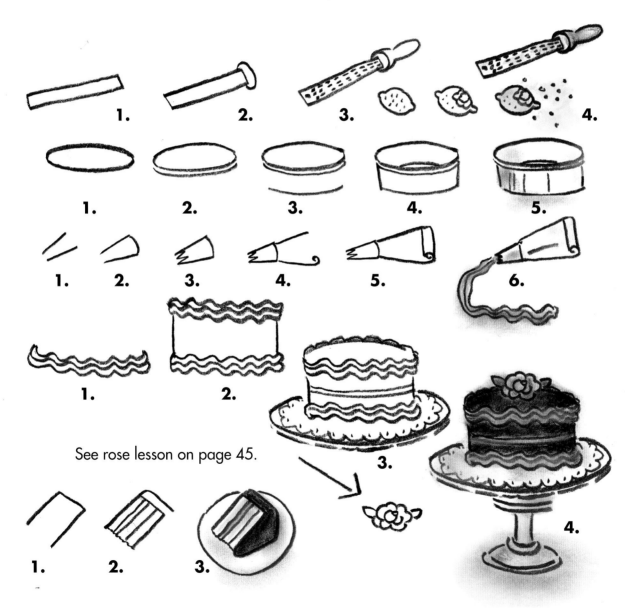

1.   2.   3.   4.

1.   2.   3.   4.   5.

1.   2.   3.   4.   5.   6.

1.   2.

See rose lesson on page 45.

3.

1.   2.   3.   4.

How to Draw
Little Man Licking His Paws

Bonus: recipe for escargot

½ stick butter or
2 tablespoons olive oil for sautéing
24 snails
1 tablespoon fresh garlic, minced
1 tablespoon fresh basil, minced

Sauté snails in butter with garlic and
basil until tender (8 to 10 minutes).

Fact: Snails are dee-lish!

1.　　**2.**　　**3.**　　**4.**

Yum! Little Man eats all of his escargot.

Jars, Bottles, and a Recycling Barrel

1.   2.   3.   1.   2.   3.

1.   2.   3.

CRASH!
CLINK!
CHINK!

1.   2.   3.

How to Draw a
Delivery Truck

BONG BONG
BONG BONG
BONG

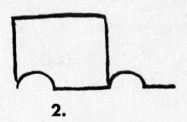
1.

Across town, bells ring five times because it's five o'clock in the morning.

2.

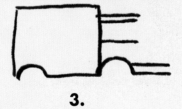
3.

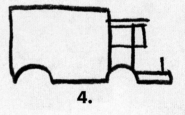
4.

5.

6.

7.

How to Draw
Restaurant Kittens, Feasting on Goodies

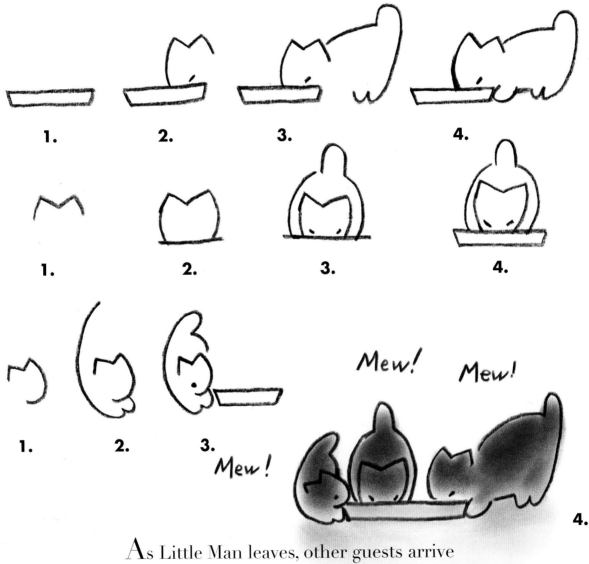

1. **2.** **3.** **4.**

1. **2.** **3.** **4.**

1. **2.** **3.**

Mew! Mew!

Mew!

4.

As Little Man leaves, other guests arrive
at Le Chat Noir to enjoy a good meal.

As Little Man scampers back along the woodland path, he passes a fairy ring of mushrooms.

How to Draw
Woodland Mushrooms

Glow-in-the-Dark Mushroom

Puffball

1.

2.

3.

Toadstool
(Also see Toad on page 90.)

1.

2.

3.

4.

5.

6.

7.

Bonus: A slug with silvery trail

Boletus Mushroom

1.

2.

3.

4.

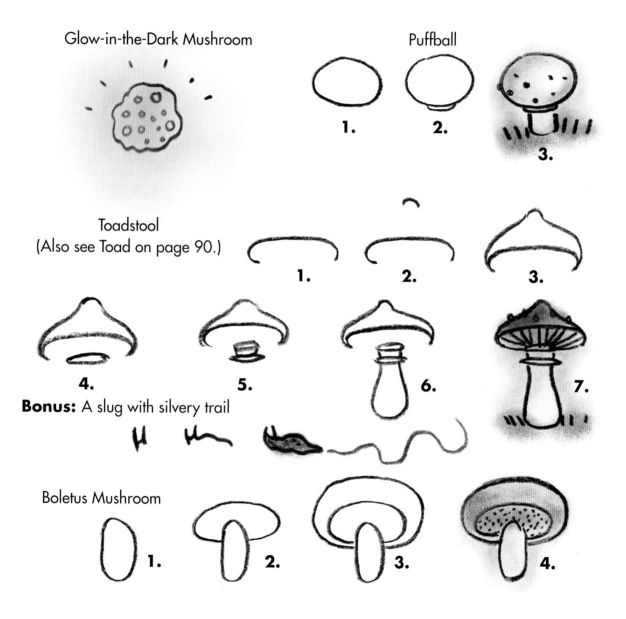

How to Draw a
Toad

1.

2.

3.

4.

5.

6.

7.

KA-LOOMPF!

8.

9.

How to Draw a
Fishing Boat at Dawn

A chilly wind rustles Scarecrow's straw, twisting him around as if to greet Little Man on his return home through the pumpkin patch.

"You see? He won't even touch his cat food. That's because he was out hunting on Halloween night!"

Back in his comfy chair, Little Man dreams of his nighttime friends and of having another delicious dish of escargot.

Index

PING!

PONK!

WIN

How to Draw a
Pencil, Sharpener, and Pastels

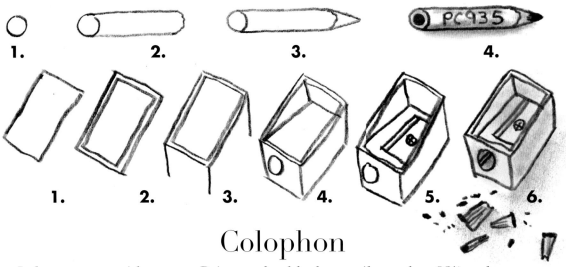

1.   2.   3.   4.

1.   2.   3.   4.   5.   6.

Colophon

I always carry with me my Prismacolor black pencil number 935 and a sharpener. I used a set of pastel chalks to color my drawings. When my chalks crumbled, which chalks always do, I used my fingers or a paintbrush to apply the chalk dust to my drawings. Didot and Futura are the book's typefaces, the very same ones that I used in my previous book, *How to Draw a Sailing Cat*. Special thanks to Mina Chung and Magdalena Nemesh.

About the Authors

Joy Sikorski and Nick Sunday have collaborated on several How to Draw books, including *How to Draw a Sailing Cat,* *How to Draw a Radish,* and *Squeaky Chalk and Other Fun Things to Draw.* Visit www.joyradish.com for more information about the How to Draw books.

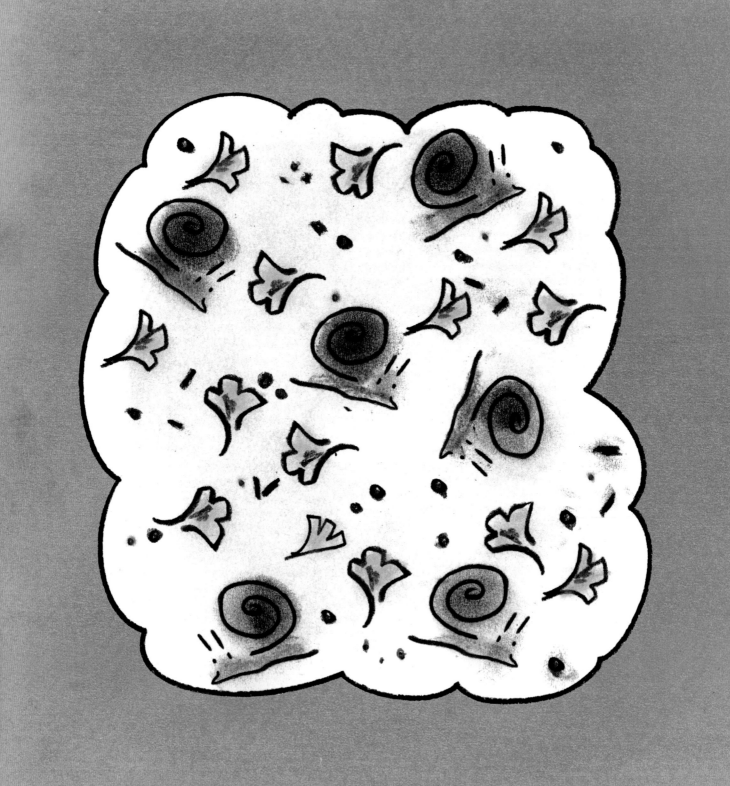